SCENE BY SCENE
COMPARATIVE WORKBOOK HL17

The King's Speech
by Tom Hooper

Theme/Issue - Relationships

Literary Genre

General Vision and Viewpoint

Copyright © 2016 by Amy Farrell.

All rights reserved. No part of this publication may be reproduced, distributed or transmitted in any form or by any means, including photocopying, recording, or other electronic or mechanical methods, without the prior written permission of the publisher, except in the case of brief quotations embodied in critical reviews and certain other noncommercial uses permitted by copyright law. For permission requests, write to the publisher, addressed "Attention: Permissions Coordinator," at the address below.

Scene by Scene
11 Millfield, Enniskerry
Wicklow, Ireland.
www.scenebysceneguides.com

info@scenebysceneguides.com

The King's Speech Comparative Workbook HL17 by Amy Farrell. —1st ed.
ISBN 978-1-910949-38-2

The King's Speech Comparative Study Workbook

This workbook is designed to help Leaving Certificate English students become familiar with the Comparative Study modes and to understand how each mode may be applied to *The King's Speech*.

The Comparative Study Modes at Higher Level for 2017 are:

Theme/Issue

The theme covered in this workbook is Relationships. This theme can be applied to any relationship in a text and covers love, marriage, friendship and family bonds.

Consider the complexities of relationships and the impact they have on characters' lives.

Literary Genre

This mode refers to the way the story is told.

Consider aspects of narration such as the manner and style of narration, characterisation, setting, tension, literary techniques, etc.

The General Vision and Viewpoint

This mode refers to the author's outlook or view of life and how this viewpoint is represented in the text.

Consider whether the text is bright or dark, optimistic or pessimistic, uplifting or bleak, etc.

How Does it Work?

This workbook has three parts, one each for Theme/Issue (our chosen theme for study is Relationships), Literary Genre and General Vision and Viewpoint. Each part has three sections: Know the Text, Know the Mode and Compare the Texts.

Know The Text

These questions are on *The King's Speech* text and refer specifically to this film. Through answering these questions you will get to know the text well, while also getting a feel for the Comparative Study mode the questions relate to.

Know the Mode

These questions use 'mode' specific terms and phrases and are intended to help prepare you for tackling exam questions. They focus on the mode itself, rather than the text you have studied. You apply your knowledge of the text to the mode in question.

Compare the Texts

These questions ask you to compare your texts under specific aspects of each mode. It is important that you get used to the idea of comparing and contrasting your chosen texts, as this is what the Comparative Study is all about. It is good practice to think about your texts in terms of their similarities and differences within each mode.

This approach is designed to prevent 'drift' between modes and focuses on analysis and personal response, rather than summary.

Theme/Issue - Know the Text

1 What are your first impressions of Bertie and Elizabeth's marriage?

2 Does Elizabeth care about and understand her husband? Give examples to support your view.

3 Does Bertie care about and understand his wife? Give examples to support your view.

4 What **strengths** do you see in Bertie and Elizabeth's marriage?

5 What **weaknesses** or problems do you see in Bertie and Elizabeth's marriage?

6 Is this a positive or negative relationship? Use examples to justify your view.

| 7 | Are Bertie and Elizabeth a good match? |

| 8 | Is their relationship important to Elizabeth and Bertie? |

KNOW THE TEXT

9 Describe Bertie's relationship with his father.

10 What causes problems in this relationship?

THE KING'S SPEECH – THEME/ISSUE – RELATIONSHIPS

11 Is this a positive or negative relationship?

12 Describe Bertie's relationship with his brother, David.

KNOW THE TEXT

13 What causes problems in this relationship?

14 Is this a positive or negative relationship?

THE KING'S SPEECH – THEME/ISSUE – RELATIONSHIPS

15 Overall, are Bertie's relationships with his family positive or negative?

16 How does Bertie treat his children?

KNOW THE TEXT

17 How well do Bertie and Lionel get along at first?

18 What barriers are there to their friendship?

THE KING'S SPEECH – THEME/ISSUE – RELATIONSHIPS

| 19 | How does their relationship **change** and **develop**? |

| 20 | What **strengths** do you see in this friendship? |

KNOW THE TEXT

21 What **weaknesses** or **problems** do you see in this friendship?

22 Is this a positive or negative relationship?

23   Is this relationship important to Bertie and Lionel?

24   Does their friendship bring them happiness?

Theme/Issue - Know the Mode

25 Are relationships in this text generally **positive** (warm, supportive, nurturing, genuine) or **negative** (cold, cruel, destructive, false)?

THE KING'S SPEECH - THEME/ISSUE - RELATIONSHIPS

> **26** What makes relationships in this text complicated and **difficult**?

KNOW THE MODE

27 What would **improve** relationships in this text?

28 How do relationships **change** during the story?

29 What did **you learn** about relationships from watching this film?

30 Are relationships **portrayed realistically** in this text? Make use of examples to support the points you make.

KNOW THE MODE

31 Are relationships in this story **interesting** and **involving**?

32 Did anything about the theme of relationships in this text **shock, upset** or **unsettle** you?

33 What is the **most signficant relationship** in this text?
What makes it so significant and important?

THE KING'S SPEECH – THEME/ISSUE – RELATIONSHIPS

34 Do relationships in this story bring characters **happiness** or **sorrow**?

KNOW THE MODE

35 Choose **key moments** from this story that highlight relationships in the text.

Theme/Issue - Compare the Texts

36 Were relationships in *The King's Speech* more positive and supportive than the relationships in your other texts? Give specific examples.

THE KING'S SPEECH – THEME/ISSUE – RELATIONSHIPS

37 Rank the relationships you have studied in your various texts from most positive to most negative. Add a note to explain your choices.

38 Were relationships in *The King's Speech* the most engaging and interesting that you have studied? Explain your choice.

THE KING'S SPEECH - THEME/ISSUE - RELATIONSHIPS

> **39** Rank the relationships you have studied in your various texts from most interesting to least interesting. Add a note to explain your choices.

40 Did you **learn most** about the theme of relationships from this text or another text on your comparative course?

41 What **similarities** do you notice in the theme of relationships in this text and your other comparative texts?

COMPARE THE TEXTS

42

What differences do you notice in the theme of relationships in this text and your other comparative texts?

COMPARE THE TEXTS

THE KING'S SPEECH - LITERARY GENRE

Literary Genre - Know the Text

43   How is this story told? (Consider the film format).

44   Why is the story told in this way?
          What is the effect of this?

KNOW THE TEXT

45 What was your initial view of Bertie?

46 How does Hooper develop Bertie's character?

47 What was your initial view of Lionel?

48 How does Hooper develop Lionel's character?

KNOW THE TEXT

49 What is the effect of seeing so many scenes where Bertie and Lionel practise together?

50 What is your opinion of Elizabeth, Bertie's wife?

THE KING'S SPEECH - LITERARY GENRE

51 What made you like the characters of Bertie, Lionel and Elizabeth?

52 What made you dislike Bertie's Father and his brother, David?

53 What makes the swearing scene funny? How does it add to the story?

54 What **music** is used in the soundtrack? How does this contribute to the movie?

THE KING'S SPEECH – LITERARY GENRE

55 Is this a film about duty, friendship, bravery or something else?

56 Comment on the **costumes** in the film. How do they help to tell the story?

KNOW THE TEXT

57 How does the **historical aspect** contribute to the storytelling here?

58 Does the fact that many characters are **royalty** add to the story in any way?

59 In its review, *The New York Post* called this film an "immense crowd-pleaser." Do you agree with this comment? What **different aspects** of the text **combine** to make the audience feel this way?

Literary Genre - Know the Mode

60 Did **you** enjoy the **storyline** of the text?
Was it exciting/compelling/tense/emotional?
Why/why not?

61 Is there just one **plot** or many plots?
What connections can you make between the storylines?

62 What three things interested **you** most in the story?

63 Are **characters** vivid, realistic and well-developed?

64 Do **you** empathise or **identify** with any character(s)?
Did you become involved in this story or care about the characters? Use examples.

65 Who was your **favourite character**?
What aspects of this character did you enjoy?

66 Consider Bertie as the film's **hero**. What made Bertie a **memorable** or **interesting** character?

67 Who was your **least favourite character**? What aspects of this character did you dislike? What made them a memorable or interesting character?

68 Is the story humorous or tragic, romantic or realistic? Explain using examples.

69 To what **genre** does it belong?
What aspects of this genre did **you** enjoy?
Is it Romance, Thriller, Horror, Action/Adventure, Historical, Fantasy, Science-fiction, Satire, etc.?

70 How does the director create **suspense, high emotion** and **excitement** in the text? What **techniques** does he use to good advantage?

71 Consider the director's use of **tension** and **resolution** in the film. What are the major **tensions/problems/conflicts** in the text? Are they **resolved** or not?

| 72 | Did the director make use of any striking patterns of **imagery** or **symbols** to add to the story? |

| 73 | How does the director make use of the **unexpected** in this text? What did this add to the story? (Think about key moments here.) |

KNOW THE MODE

74 What is the **climax** (high point) of the story?

75 What did **you** think of this moment?
How did it make **you feel**?

| **76** | Comment on the **language** of the film. How does this spoken dimension add to the story? |

| **77** | Comment on the **pacing** of the film. How does this add to the story? |

KNOW THE MODE

78 Comment on the **setting** of the film.
Consider time, place, and specific locations such as Buckingham Palace. How does setting add to your understanding of the characters and their story?

THE KING'S SPEECH - LITERARY GENRE

79 Was anything about this film **moving** or **emotional**?
Think of moments in the film that you responded to. What made them moving? How did this add to the story?

KNOW THE MODE

80 On a scale of one to ten, how much did you enjoy the **ending**? What was satisfying/unsatisfying about it? Was anything left unanswered?

81 The experiences of seeing a play, reading a novel and viewing a film are very different.
What aspects of the **film form** worked well in this story, in your opinion?

82 What did **you** like about **the way** the story was told?
*Mention aspects of storytelling and literary techniques that **you** found enjoyable. Refer to key moments.*

THE KING'S SPEECH - LITERARY GENRE

83 Identify **key moments** in the film that illustrate Literary Genre (the way the story is told). Clearly **define literary techniques/aspects of narrative** in your analysis.

KNOW THE MODE

Literary Genre - Compare the Texts

84 Did **you** like the way this story was told more than your other comparative texts?
State what you enjoyed most about each.

85

Is *The King's Speech* more **exciting** than your other texts?

Consider tension, pacing, suspense, conflict and the unexpected.

86 Are **characters** more engaging in this film than in your other texts?
Refer to each of your texts in you answer.

87

Is the **setting** more effective in telling this story than in your other texts?
Refer to each of your texts in your answer.

88 Is this story more **unpredictable** than your other texts?
Refer to each of your texts in your answer.

89 Did this film have greater **emotional power** than your other texts?
Was emotional power created in a more interesting way here or in a different text?

THE KING'S SPEECH - LITERARY GENRE

90 What **similarities** do you notice in the Literary Genre of this film and your other comparative texts?
Mention specific aspects of narrative.

COMPARE THE TEXTS

91 What **differences** do you notice in the Literary Genre of this film and your other comparative texts?
Mention specific aspects of narrative.

THE KING'S SPEECH - GENERAL VISION AND VIEWPOINT

General Vision and Viewpoint - Know the Text

92 Do Bertie and Elizabeth love and support one another? Is their marriage a positive or negative comment on life?

93 Is Bertie under a lot of pressure in this film? Rank the three things that put him under the most pressure or stress.
Think about his role as King and his relationships with his family and the public.

KNOW THE TEXT

> **94** How do **you** feel watching Bertie's early attempts at public speaking?

> **95** Did you want Bertie to succeed?
> What made you wish for his success?

96 Does privilege and celebrity bring the Royal Family happiness?
What does this tell us about life?

97 What does his friendship with Lionel add to Bertie's life?

KNOW THE TEXT

> **98** How does war looming in the background add to the atmosphere?

> **99** David abdicates in order to marry for love.
> Is this seen as a romantic gesture?
> What does this suggest about life?

THE KING'S SPEECH - GENERAL VISION AND VIEWPOINT

100 Why do Bertie and Lionel argue in Westminster Cathedral? How do you feel watching this scene?

101 Did you ever truly fear that Bertie would fail, or did you anticipate a happy ending?
Explain your answer.

KNOW THE TEXT

102 How do you feel as Bertie prepares to deliver his radio address at the end?

103 How does the closing section make you feel?
Use 'I' statements to develop your Personal Response.

THE KING'S SPEECH - GENERAL VISION AND VIEWPOINT

104 Is Bertie's future promising?

105 How does a **happy ending** reflect Hooper's view of life?

KNOW THE TEXT

106 The Wall Street Journal described this as, "a film that makes your spirit soar."
Is this an accurate statement?

107 What is Tom Hooper telling us about life in this story?
What is Tom Hooper's message?
Is his outlook positive or negative, in your view?

General Vision and Viewpoint - Know the Mode

108 Identify bright/hopeful/optimistic aspects of the film.

109 Identify dark/hopeless/pessimistic aspects of the film.

> **110** Is this text **optimistic** or **pessimistic**? Explain. *Consider characters' happiness, imagery, atmosphere, future prospects, etc.*

> **111** On a scale of one to ten, how optimistic is this text?

112 Identify the **aspects of life** that the director concentrates on.
Are they positive or negative?
Consider overcoming adversity, isolation, bravery, determination, loyalty, etc.

THE KING'S SPEECH - GENERAL VISION AND VIEWPOINT

113 What **comments** do characters make on their **society** and the problems they're facing?

KNOW THE MODE

114 Are characters happy or unhappy?

115 What makes characters in this story happy and fulfilled?

THE KING'S SPEECH - GENERAL VISION AND VIEWPOINT

116 What makes characters in this story unhappy and unfulfilled?

117 Are **relationships** destructive or nurturing? What do they reveal about life, as we see characters supported/thwarted in their efforts to grow/mature?

118 Are **imagery** and **language** bright or dark in the text? (Tone of the text)

119 What is the **mood** of this text?

120 What does this story **teach us about life?**
What do we learn about life's hardships? Are struggles overcome? Is determination rewarded? Is life difficult or joyful?

121 How do you **feel** as you watch this film?
Refer to key moments to anchor your answer.

KNOW THE MODE

122 How do you **feel** at the **end**?

123 Are **questions** raised by the text **resolved** by the end?
Are they resolved **happily** or **unhappily**?

124 Are **you hopeful** or **despairing** regarding the prospects for human **happiness** in this story?
Are characters likely to be happy?

125 Identify the **key moments** in the film that illustrate the General Vision and Viewpoint of the text.

KNOW THE MODE

General Vision and Viewpoint - Compare the Texts

126 Is life happier for characters in this story than in your other comparative texts? Explain.

COMPARE THE TEXTS

127 Do characters in this text face more obstacles and difficulties than in your other texts?
Who struggles most?

128 Are characters in this text **rewarded more** for their struggles than in your other texts?
By overcoming adversity, do they achieve true happiness and contentment in a way that is not realised in your other texts?

129 Is this the brightest, most hopeful and triumphant text you have studied? Explain why its message is more or less positive than your other texts.

130 Which of your chosen texts was the bleakest and most upsetting or depressing?
Explain why it was more negative than your other texts. What made them more positive?

131 Plot your three texts on a scale of one to ten, from darkest (most pessimistic) to brightest (most optimistic). Add points to explain their position.

THE KING'S SPEECH - GENERAL VISION AND VIEWPOINT

132 What **similarities** do you notice in the General Vision and Viewpoint of this text and your other comparative texts?

COMPARE THE TEXTS

133 What **differences** do you notice in the General Vision and Viewpoint of this text and your other comparative texts?

www.ingramcontent.com/pod-product-compliance
Lightning Source LLC
Chambersburg PA
CBHW050714090526
44587CB00019B/3374